On the Trail of Henry Hudson and Our Dutch Heritage

Through the Municipal Seals in New York 1609 to 2009

Second Edition

Compiled by Marvin W. Bubie

Square Circle Press
Schenectady, New York

On the Trail of Henry Hudson
and Our Dutch Heritage
Through the Municipal Seals of New York
1609 to 2009

Published by
Square Circle Press LLC
PO Box 913
Schenectady, NY 12301
www.squarecirclepress.com

©2009, 2014 by Marvin W. Bubie.
All rights reserved. No part of this publication may be reproduced or transmitted in any form or by any means, electronic or mechanical, except brief quotes extracted for the purpose of book reviews or similar articles, without permission in writing from the publisher.

First edition 2009, privately published.
Revised second edition, 2014.
Printed and bound in the United States of America on acid-free, durable paper.
ISBN 13: 978-0-9856926-5-0
ISBN 10: 0-9856926-5-0
Library of Congress Control Number: 2014954141

Cover design created by Richard Vang, ©2014, Square Circle Press.
Front cover: The image used for the seal is a photograph by Richard Vang, of Henry Hudson's ship, the Half Moon, taken just south of Albany during the flotilla that commemorated the 400th anniversary of the explorer's voyage up the Hudson River. Photograph ©2009, Square Circle Press.
Back cover: Stained glass representation of the Half Moon, created for the municipal buildings of the Town of Halfmoon.
Title page: Representation of the Half Moon on a thread painted quilt, created by Barbara Brown for the Town of Stuyvesant for the Hudson-Fulton-Champlain Quadricentennial in 2009. The image has been cropped for use on the title page.

This book is dedicated to Florence (Bubie) Hill, former Historian for the Town of Poestenkill for 56 years. Her passion for the past inspired my interest in history, genealogy and in writing. She was the author of several books about her hometown.

Contents

Preface, vii

New York City, 3
    Borough of Manhattan, 4
    Borough of Staten Island, 5
    Borough of Brooklyn, 6
    Borough of Queens, 7
    The Bronx, 8
Nassau County, 9
    Town of Oyster Bay, 10
Westchester County
    City of Yonkers, 11
    Village of Tarrytown, 12
    Village of Sleepy Hollow, 13
    City of Peekskill, 14
Rockland County, 15
    Town of Haverstraw, 16
Orange County, 17
Dutchess County, 18
    Town of Fishkill, 19
    City of Poughkeepsie, 20
    Town of Hyde Park, 21
    Town of Rhinebeck, 23
Ulster County, 24
    City of Kingston, 25
    Village of Saugerties, 27
Columbia County, 28
    City of Hudson, 29
    Town of Clavarack, 30
    Town of Kinderhook, 32
    Village of Kinderhook, 35
    Village of Valatie, 36
    Town of Stuyvesant, 37
Greene County, 38
    Village of Catskill, 39

Albany County, 40
    Town of Rensselaerville, 41
    Town of Bethlehem, 42
    Town of New Scotland, 43
    Town of Guilderland, 44
    Town of Colonie, 46
    City of Albany, 47
    City of Watervliet, 50
    City of Cohoes, 51
Rensselaer County, 52
    Town of Schodack, 53
    Town of Nassau, 54
    Village of Nassau, 55
    Town of Stephentown, 56
    Town of Sand Lake, 57
    City of Rensselaer, 58
    Town of North Greenbush, 59
    Town of Poestenkill, 60
    City of Troy, 61
    Town of Hoosick, 62
    Town of Pittstown, 63
    Town of Schaghticoke, 64
Saratoga County
    Village of Waterford, 65
    Town of Halfmoon, 66
    Town of Clifton Park, 67
Schenectady County, 69
    Town of Niskayuna, 70
    City of Schenectady, 71
    Town of Rotterdam, 72
    Village of Scotia, 73
Montgomery County
    City of Amsterdam, 74

Seals as Subjects for Works of Art, 75
Acknowledgments, 76
About the Author, 79

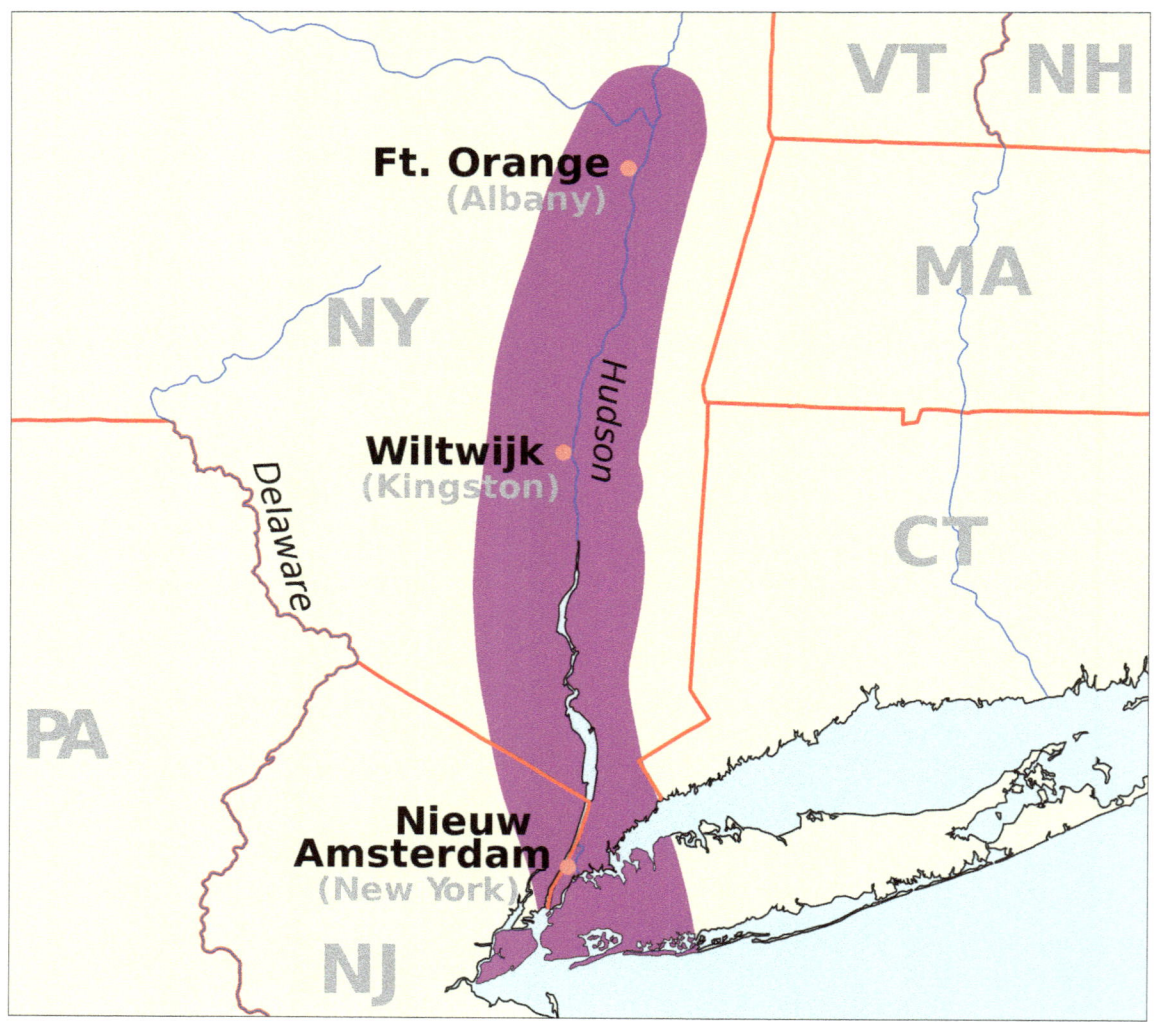

New Netherland, ca. 1650. This has been cropped from the original, *Karte von Neu-Niederland und Neu-Schweden etwa 1650* (Map of New-Nederland and New-Sweden ca. 1650), available on the WikiMedia Commons web site. Though it is a modern representation and seems to be somewhat controversial, it gives an excellent representation of the geographic region covered in this book.

Preface

The Hudson River Valley has a distinct heritage in New York and the rest of the United States. In addition to the usual background from the larger European countries, we also have a unique Dutch heritage.

Our Dutch heritage is expressed in many ways, such as through the names of our municipalities, universities, and the people listed in the phone books. Albany celebrates the Tulip Festival annually, and the "Dutchman's Shoes" trophy is awarded to the winner of the annual football game between Rensselaer Polytechnic Institute and Union College.

Another way we express our heritage is through official municipal seals. Our elected government leaders conduct official business and press conferences from behind podiums with official seals on them. Larger versions can be found in the Council Chambers or Judicial Chambers, where legal decisions are made. Seals are also found on the official government letterheads, web sites, and even on the police and fire vehicles.

Municipal seals have existed since biblical times. Although the earliest purpose of seals was to prevent identity fraud, these days seals are used for branding much like a corporate logo. Some municipalities simply choose a logo and use it as they would use a seal. The old seal may be kept for official government letterhead, business cards, etc., but the logo is used for identifying government property, including vehicles. Some designs originally made on wax do not print well on paper or when enlarged as is commonly done today. Over time, some municipalities might decide that the original brand is no longer appropriate and choose another one. Other municipalities never change their seal, choosing instead to honor a heritage even if it reflects a bygone era.

As residents, we often get to choose our seals through our Board of Supervisors or Town Councils. Therefore, in this area of New York, you will find windmills, illustrations of a 17th century sailing ship, and unique Dutch names, such as Rensselaer, Watervliet, Stuyvesant, Yonkers, and Kinderhook. 400 years after Henry Hudson and 345 years after the Dutch formally relinquished claim to New York, the Dutch influence is both subtle and pervasive. This influence is a part of our daily lives.

This book is a result of a project that got out of hand. Growing up in the Albany-Troy-Schenectady area, I have always known something about our unique Dutch heritage. When researching the various municipal seals, I found more than I expected. While I have tried to include those municipalities that have a Dutch name, or that have some Dutch symbolism in their seal, or those communities that were founded by the Dutch, I may have missed some. Some communities along the Hudson River claim other than a Dutch heritage. Others have had significant Revolutionary War events depicted on their seals. Some depict industrial or agricultural themes. For example, Cohoes, Peekskill, and Poughkeepsie all have seals that do not illustrate any Dutch symbols, but were settled by the Dutch. Each seal is a mini history lesson and a collection of symbols, and all relate to and speak of a common heritage. These seals seem to indicate we owe a lot more to the Dutch than is commonly taught. So, if there was still a significant Dutch heritage, I chose to be inclusive.

The order in which the municipalities appear in this Second Edition follows a general route of "discovery," north and west up the Hudson River and beyond, from New York City to the City of Amsterdam in Montgomery County. Within the counties, the same route is generally followed, and while it is not a perfect pattern, it provides a leisurely flow up through the Hudson Valley and into the more interior municipalities where the Dutch heritage is still represented.

The inclusion of any municipal seal does not imply endorsement of this book in any way. In addition, many of the seals included are protected by copyright and permission was required prior to their use. And, unfortunately, a good clear image was not always obtainable or did not even exist for some municipalities. In other cases, the official seal is black and white, but a color seal is used on municipal vehicles and the like, and which are usually much more interesting to look at. In all cases, the best available images were used in this book.

Marvin Bubie
2009, revised 2014

On the Trail of Henry Hudson and Our Dutch Heritage

New York City

New York City has one of the oldest seals having adopted it in 1686. Therefore, it is one of the seals which, on official record, follows the ancient rules of heraldry, but the text below has been revised into more common language. It contains an illustration of the beaver similar to the earlier seal of New Amsterdam. The beaver was of primary economic importance to New Netherland.

The coat of arms are displayed upon a shield, with the sails of a windmill in a diagonal cross. Two beavers are between the sails, above and below, and on each side is a flour barrel.

Supporting the shield is a sailor, who holds a plummet in his right hand, his left arm supporting the top of the shield. Above his right shoulder is a cross-staff. On the other side is a brave of the Lenni Lenape of Manhattan, his right arm supporting top of the shield, his left hand holding the upper end of a bow, the lower end of which rests on the ground. The shield and the supporters rest upon a horizontal laurel branch.

The date of 1625, beneath the horizontal laurel branch is the year of the establishment of New Amsterdam.

Upon the crest is an American eagle with wings displayed, upon a hemisphere. The eagle replaced the British crown in 1783.

The legend is a ribbon encircling the lower half of the design, with the words *SIGILLUM CIVITATIS NOVI EBORACI*, Latin for "Seal of the City of New York."

The whole is encircled by a laurel wreath.

Borough of Manhattan

In addition to the seal of New York City, each of the five boroughs has its own administration, each with a President of the Borough and of course, their own flag and their own seal. The Borough of Manhattan is coterminous with New York County.

The seal of Manhattan is very similar to the seal of New York City, with a crest showing windmill blade, beaver, and barrels of flour. The Dutch sailor and Native American also appear as does the American eagle on a hemisphere. The laurel wreath is not included and the date on the seal is November 1, 1683. This is the date when New York City was divided into wards, Manhattan being one of them.

Borough of Staten Island

Although its origins are unclear, the symbolism on this seal is magnificent.

In 1609 Henry Hudson named the island *Staaten Eyelandt* in honor of the Dutch Parliament, or "States General." The Borough of Richmond was created from the County of Richmond in 1898 during the consolidation of Greater New York. The kissing doves on the shield recall the same birds in the center of the county seal (below). Lady Liberty holds the shield, which also includes an "R" for Richmond and an "S" for *signum*. In the background is Henry Hudson's ship, *Halve Maen* (Half Moon), with a half moon in the sky above it. The rowboat might be an oyster skiff or one of Hudson's rowboats that carried men ashore.

The borough was renamed as Staten Island in 1977. At the time of this revision, borough officials are considering replacing a recent, modern logo with the older seal above.

Borough of Brooklyn

The village was authorized in 1646 and The Dutch Reform Church of Flatland was formed in 1654. Brooklyn was a city in its own right when it became a part of New York City in 1898. Brooklyn is the most populous of the boroughs of New York, with over 2.2 million people.

Within the seal appears a figure of the goddess of justice in gold, holding Roman *fasces* in her left hand, set on a background of light blue.

Encircling her figure on a background of dark blue appear the words *Een Draght Mackt Maght*, the old Dutch motto for "In Unity There Is Strength." The outside trim of the seal is gold.

Borough of Queens

Two flowers, the tulip and the rose, are surrounded by a circle of wampum, which is taken from the Indian name for Long Island, *Seawanhaka*, or "island of sea shells." The first settlers are represented by the flowers: the tulip, emblematic of the Dutch; the double red and white rose of the English, representing the Houses of York and Lancaster. The Queen's Crown signifies the name of the county and borough in honor of Queen Catherine of Braganza, wife of Charles II, King of England. The date indicates the year in which Queens County became a part of the City of New York on January 1, 1898.

The Bronx

The Bronx Flag contains the same three horizontal stripes as the colonial Dutch flag.

In the center, and extending into the orange stripe above and the blue stripe below, is the Bronck family crest, encircled by a laurel wreath. The laurel denotes honor and fame.

The crest in the center of the laurel wreath bears an eagle on a hemisphere, facing eastward with its wings displayed. This represents the hope of the New World, while not forgetting the Old.

Below this is a three-pointed shield on which is the face of the sun, with rays displayed, rising from the sea. This signifies the coming of peace and liberty and the importance of commerce. Below the shield is a ribbon, on which is the motto, *NE CEDE MALIS*, Latin for "Yield Not To Evil," a perfect civic slogan.

Nassau County

On Jan 3, 1899, the first resolution of the Nassau County Board of Supervisors was for a county coat of arms, seal, and flag, and to use the same design used by the House of Nassau, Netherlands. Although there are several instances where it is recorded that American municipalities requested permission from the government of the Netherlands to use their seal for their own, there is no mention in this case.

The seal includes a coat of arms upon a blue shield, with a lion rampant between seven billets. The colors are taken from the Dutch flag.

Town of Oyster Bay

The diary of Dutch voyager David deVries includes an entry for June 4, 1639, which states that his ship anchored in a haven on the north of *Lange Eylandt* (Long Island). The sailors found many fine oysters there, from which the town derives its name. The seal features a seagull on a gold-yellow (sometimes orange) background. The seagull was drawn by Oyster Bay artist Alfred J. Walker, who went on to become an artist with the Walt Disney Studios.

Sagamore Hill in Oyster Bay was the home of Theodore Roosevelt, 26th President of the United States, who was of Dutch heritage. He lived there from 1886 until his death in 1919.

City of Yonkers

In the late 1640s (about 20 years after Peter Minuit bought Manhattan Island), Adriaen Van der Donck received a grant of land from the Dutch East India Company which he called *Colon Donck* (Donck's Colony). He built one of the first saw mills in the New World, at the junction of the Hudson and Nepperhan Rivers. Van der Donck was referred to as *Jonk Herr*, "young gentleman" or "young nobleman," by reason of his status in Holland. These words evolved through several changes into "the Jonk Heer's land," "The Younckers," "The Yonkers," and finally to the present iteration of "Yonkers." The city was incorporated in 1872.

The new official logo is a deliberate re-branding of the city and was the result of a contest won by Karen Brochart. It was adopted by the City Council on Oct 23, 2012.

Village of Tarrytown

The first settlers were Dutch. The area was suitable for growing wheat and it was called "Terve Town," which was mispronounced as Tarrytown.

The seal depicts the capture of Major John André by John Paulding, David Williams, and Isaac Van Wart, all citizens of Tarrytown. This event prevented Benedict Arnold from succeeding in his plan to capture West Point, a potential disaster for the Continental Army in the American War for Independence.

Village of Sleepy Hollow

In 1655 Adriaen Van der Donck, a Dutch colonist, first published a work which referred to the Pocantico River as *Slapershaven* or, literally, "Sleepers' Haven." Sleepy Hollow appears to be a later, anglicized version of this name and actually applied to the valley of the Pocantico River. It now serves as the name of the incorporated village.

In the late 1790s Washington Irving came to visit his friend and relative, James K. Paulding, in Tarrytown. Together the two young men explored the area of Sleepy Hollow, hunting and fishing and talking with local folk. The fruits of Irving's visits were later to be immortalized in the story, "The Legend of Sleepy Hollow." In it the father of American literature drew heavily from Sleepy Hollow's landscape and customs.

City of Peekskill

The Peekskill region was known to the Dutch as "Jan Peeck's kill," and to the English as "John Peak's Creek." This name was adapted from the explorer and fur businessman Jan Peeck. Thus, Mr. Peeck, or Peak, or Peek (according to various spellings), and the Dutch word for stream or creek, (*kill* or *kil*) were combined as this place name. In 1685 the written deed transfer of land for these items was the Ryck's Patent. The seal depicts the industry that came later in history.

Rockland County

In the early 1600s, some of the earliest Dutch settlers—eager to escape the "city life" of the New Amsterdam colony—moved to Rockland (then part of Orange County). During the first half of the century, they cleared the land, built homes, schools, and churches. Many of those farms, in the same family since the 1600s, still exist there.

The oldest surviving structure in the county is the De Wint House, built in 1700 and named after the family who owned it during the American Revolution, when George Washington visited there several times. It is an outstanding example of Dutch Colonial architecture, and is currently maintained by the Grand Lodge of Free and Accepted Masons of the State of New York.

Town of Haverstraw

In 1609 Henry Hudson sailed his ship just north of what is now Albany, and on the return trip the Half Moon anchored in what is now Haverstraw Bay, the widest point in the river. Haverstraw is one of the oldest names in the geography of North America. The word is Dutch and it first appeared on a map in 1616. It was originally written *Haverstroo* and means "oat straw," descriptive of the waving straw of the river meadows.

At the time of this second edition in 2014, the Town of Haverstraw website displays a seal of the Half Moon sailing the Hudson River. What is truly interesting is that this seal is animated; the ship sails towards the viewer from the background of the seal. It is one of a handful of animated seals in America.

Orange County

Orange County was established in 1683 as one of the original counties of the Province of New York. The county name is derived primarily after Prince William III, Stadtholder of the House of Orange-Nassau of the Dutch Republic. After the death of England's Queen Mary, he took the throne as William III of England. The name was meant to honor both England and the Netherlands. This seal has been in use at least since the late 1700s.

Dutchess County

One of the original counties formed in Colonial New York in 1683, the county seal is also one of New York State's oldest.

From 1683 to 1725 most of the settlers in Dutchess County were Dutch. Many of these moved in from Albany and Ulster Counties.

Like other early seals with agricultural themes, the seal is representative of a plow and stems of ripened wheat.

Town of Fishkill

In 1683, nineteen years after the Dutch surrendered New Amsterdam to the English, Frances Rombout and Gulian Verplanck purchased 85,000 acres in Dutchess County from the Wappinger Indians. Their house, built about 1709, still stands in Beacon, and is the oldest continuous residence in Dutchess County. The name Fishkill is derived from two Dutch words: *vis* (fish) and *kill* (creek or stream).

City of Poughkeepsie

The first settlers were Dutch, and among the first, if not the first, was Baltus Van Kleeck. Founded in 1687, the community became an incorporated village in 1799, and the city was chartered in 1854. Poughkeepsie was the state capital of New York from 1777 through 1783. In 1788, New York State ratified the United States Constitution at the Market Street courthouse. The beehive as a city symbol is one of the oldest in the world, dating back to biblical times.

Town of Hyde Park

Hyde Park was originally settled by Jacobus Stoutenburg, of Dutch descent, in 1742 and was known at that time by the family name. He was a descendant of Peter van Stoutenburg of Amersfoot, Pays d'Utrecht, Netherlands. His most notable position was the first Treasurer of New Amsterdam (New York City). The town was officially named Hyde Park in 1812. Its seals provide a perfect example of the development of seals and municipal logos in American life.

The new seal above was adopted officially in 2014. It celebrates the iconic view of the Hudson River from Hyde Park, long enjoyed by artists, residents, and visitors to the Vanderbilt Mansion National Historic Site. It features a stone wall with daffodils in the foreground, a distinctive feature of the town, along with Henry Hudson's ship the Half Moon, and a border of stars symbolizing the 32nd U.S. President, Franklin D. Roosevelt.

The seal was designed and created by Town Historian Carol Kohan and graphics designer Yvonne Laube.

As a way to present a town seal that would be more easily recognized by the public as representative of the multiple facets of modern Hyde Park, the town went from a more traditional heraldic seal, to one that is more of a tool for corporate branding. Since 1964, the seal had been a composite coat of arms of two of the town's founding families, the Stoutenburgs and the Roosevelts. It was designed by then Town Historian Beatrice Frederiksen and Reverend Gordon Kidd of St. James Episcopal Church, and drawn by Albert McClure, curator with the National Park Service. The older seal of Hyde Park is a variation of the Stoutenburg family crest, with three roses added to represent the Roosevelt family. *Roosevelt* means "field of roses" in Dutch. Franklin Roosevelt was of Dutch lineage and he was godfather to Princess Margriet of the Netherlands, who was born in 1943. The town plans to retain the coat of arms as an important part of the town's administrative history.

In addition to this interesting history, the town has used a silhouette of FDR as their marketing logo on signs around the town. Roosevelet's home in Hyde Park is another major tourist attraction. However, with the passing of anti-smoking legislation, the image, complete with cigarette holder jutting from the President's mouth, has become somewhat controversial.

Town of Rhinebeck

The Rhinebeck town seal provides a history lesson of the town. The upper left represents the British flag and the lower right represents the Dutch flag. Settlers from both nations were early founders. The water wheel symbolizes the importance of water as an energy source to early Rhinebeck. The lower left contains violets, commemorating Rhinebeck industry. The overlay in the middle pays homage to Palatine settlers of 1710.

Ulster County

Ulster County is one of the original counties established in Colonial New York in 1683. The county was named from the Irish title of the Duke of York. In 1664 King Charles II of England granted his brother James, the Duke of York, all of New Netherland.

The current seal is a variation of the original that dates back to the colonial period. Represented in the seal are the Catskill Mountains, a sheaf of wheat, a Dutch farmer, and a Dutch stone house.

City of Kingston

In 1609, the Half Moon passed by the creek near which the future Kingston would be built. Some historians believe that, by 1614, a small trading post had been established on the Hudson near present-day Kingston. In 1652, a handful of settlers from Holland moved down from near Albany. In 1653, they arranged to purchase land from the Esopus, a tribe of the Delaware Nation, and to farm near them. On the slight promontory overlooking the flood plains, they built houses in a village that they first called Esopus, and later *Wiltwyck*, Dutch for "wild woods".

    The seal of the City of Kingston consists of a circular device with the words "City of Kingston, New York" at the top, and the date "1652" at the bottom. The Senate House represents Kingston's contribution, as first Capitol, to the history of New York State. The Catskill Mountains are a symbol of majesty and permanence. The famous Hudson River sloop reminds us of the commercial and travel purposes of the river. The sun, with its radial beams, brings a constant promise of Kingston's bright future built firmly upon a noble past. The olive branches in the outer ring of the circle depict peaceful aspirations.

Village of Saugerties

The northern boundary was roughly identified with a stream called the Sawyer's Kill, where a Dutchman named Barent Cornelis Volge operated a sawmill in the 1650s for the manor of Rensselaerswyck. The word s*augerties* means "little sawyer" in Dutch, apparently a reference to Volge.

The seal illustrates a mill with the water wheel for power.

Columbia County

The Columbia County seal was designed by Chatham artist Ron Toelke for the county's bicentennial in 1986. It is an embellished version of an earlier seal.

The central figure of Columbia, a poetic and feminine personification of the United States, symbolizes the fight for peace and justice as she holds a dove and a law book.

The clipper ship and stagecoach show how settlers came by water and land to settle in Columbia County. The ship also symbolizes the thriving whaling industry and port activity of the past.

The acorns symbolize the fertility of the land. The rope encircling the seal symbolizes the area's nautical background. An outline of mountains in the background was added to symbolize the Catskills that are visible from many parts of Columbia County.

City of Hudson

The City of Hudson is the only municipality in New York named in honor of Henry Hudson. The Dutch arrived in the 17th Century. One of them, Franz Van Hoesen, purchased a large tract of land from the Indians. His farm included the area of Hudson, plus part of what is now Greenport. Originally called Claverack Landing, it was renamed in 1785 as the City of Hudson and was the third incorporated city in the state. In the late 1700s and early 1800s Hudson was the home of a thriving whaling industry. From 1825 to 1835, whale oil was one of the city's largest exports.

    The current seal was drawn by Teri Cozza of Greenport and was adopted by the Common Council in 1979. It replaced the original seal made by Peter Maverick, a New York City silversmith, in 1785.

Town of Clavarack

According to one source, the name *claverack* is a Dutch term signifying "clover field." It was applied by Henry Hudson during his voyage upriver in 1609 when the explorer noted vast fields of white clover covering the landscape.

Claverack became a town on March 7, 1788. The seal was designed in 1984 by Florence Mossman, a local resident and the then Historian for the Town of Claverack and the County of Columbia. The seal was adopted on December 10 of that year.

The clovers were added, not because of the legend of clover fields, but because in the folklore tradition, the clover plant symbolizes good soil.

The sheaf of wheat represents the first settlers who cleared the land and established a farming community.

The bell has a two-fold meaning. First it refers to the spiritual life of the early settlers and their desire to establish a place of worship. Secondly, the bell recognizes the settlers' desire for education.

The mill wheel symbolizes the grist and saw mills that were built along the streams. They were the beginning of industry in the town.

With the withdrawal of Columbia County from Albany County in 1786, Claverack became the first seat of county government. The first courthouse was completed in 1788.

The rope signifies the town's tie to the river, when the City of Hudson was known as Claverack Landing.

Town of Kinderhook

Kinderhook was named by Henry Hudson in 1609 when he saw Indian children playing on the shores and called it *kinder hook* or "children's corner."

The first official seal of the Town of Kinderhook, formally adopted January 13, 1997, is intended to give the appearance of Dutch Delft tile. Dutch tiles usually depict scenes of Dutch life. The tiles symbolize one of the many influences the Dutch settlers had on the Town of Kinderhook.

The first tile in the first row depicts the Vanderpoel House. James Vanderpoel served as Assemblyman, County Surrogate, and was appointed Circuit Judge of the Supreme Court of the State of New York. He built this house around 1820. The Columbia County Historical Society purchased the house in 1925.

The third tile in the first row represents a mill. Mills appeared in Valatie as early as 1697. Valatie became one of the earliest industrial centers containing saw mills, grist mills, flour mills, cotton mills, plaster mills, and fulling mills. Valatie was at one time nicknamed "Millville." Nathan Wild, a prominent owner of many Valatie mills, started the first power loom that was run in New York State.

The second tile in the second row represents the Kinderhook Memorial Library. The former library was housed in the Masonic Temple, where friends donated books. In 1931, Mrs. Caroline Davie Lloyd donated the present site and in 1933, the present building was erected and was donated in memory of George Davie.

The fourth tile in the second row represents Valatie's covered bridge. The Staats Bridge, as it was called, was built in 1792 and spanned 252 feet across the creek. It is supposedly the bridge Harry Houdini lept from while making the early silent film, "Haldane of the Secret Service," in 1924.

The first tile in the third row represents a present day store front. In 1864 the building was a row of wooden buildings varying in size and architecture. In May of 1880 the entire block was destroyed by fire. After being rebuilt, it was purchased in 1882 by the Kinderhook Knitting Company, which added the brick front.

The third tile in the third row depicts the Van Alen Homestead. The house was built in 1737 and is a restored example of rural Dutch architecture. Historians believe the bricks were produced locally. Authentic tiles imported from Holland line the fireplaces of the interior.

The second tile in the fourth row depicts the First Presbyterian Church, which was built in 1877. Architects Ogden & Wright modeled the church after an old German Cathedral.

The fourth tile in the fourth row depicts Lindenwald, the home of Martin Van Buren, 8th President of the United States. (See his official portrait on the following page.) Peter Van Ness built the house in 1797. Van Buren bought the house in 1841 and added on the tower and a library.

The house derives its name from the linden trees which shelter the house from the road. He died there in 1862.

The floral tiles depict another side of the Town of Kinderhook. The second tile in the first row and the fourth tile in the third row represent the Black-eyed Susan and the Tiger Lily. These wild flowers brighten country roads and gardens throughout the town in the summer.

The fourth tile in the first row and the first tile in the fourth row represent the Violet and the Pansy. These flowers have developed from European species, just as Kinderhook has developed from European influence.

The first tile in the second row and the second tile in the third row represent the Tulip and the Daffodil. These two flowers frequent the gardens of town inhabitants in the spring. The tulip also stands as a reminder of the Dutch influence on the Town.

The third tile in the second row and the third tile in the fourth row represent an Apple Blossom and a Wheat Shaft. Apple orchards make up a fair share of the town and produce lucrative crops. The wheat shaft represents the town's agricultural background.

Birthplace of our 8th President Martin Van Buren

Village of Kinderhook

The Village of Kinderhook is most noteworthy for its native son, Martin Van Buren, the 8th President of the United States. Van Buren was born in Kinderhook in 1782 and began his road to the White House in 1821. He held the public offices of New York State Senator, Governor, and U.S. Senator. He later served as Secretary of State (1829) and Vice President (1832) in Andrew Jackson's administration. Van Buren was elected President of the United States in 1837.

He was one of only two men to serve as Vice President, Secretary of State, and President; the other is Thomas Jefferson. Van Buren was the first President to be born as an American citizen; previous Presidents were born prior to the American Revolution. He was also the only President for whom English was his second language. His native tongue was Dutch. His home, Lindenwald, appears on the Town of Kinderhook logo.

Village of Valatie

Valatie, whose name in Dutch was *Vaaltje*, means "little falls." It is named after two waterfalls on the Kinderhook Creek and the Valatie Kill.

The Dutch came to the junction of the Kinderhook and Valatie kills about 1650, trappers and hunters in search of furs, particularly beaver.

The seal honors the Beaver Cotton Mill (destroyed in 1888), significant in the history of the village.

Town of Stuyvesant

The Town of Stuyvesant was created from the Town of Kinderhook, April 21, 1823, with a territory extending along the Hudson from Rensselaer County southward to Major Abram's creek. The act forming the town provided that the first meeting be held May 6, 1823. The lower part of the town was annexed to Stockport, April 30, 1833. The name was bestowed in honor of Dutch Governor Peter Stuyvesant.

The first settlers were Swedes and Hollanders, who came soon after 1650, and bore the names of Scherbs, Scherp, Peitersen, Van Alen, Van Der Poel, Van Valkenburgh, Vosburgh, Van Alstyne, and Schermerhorn.

The logo depicts Henry Hudson's ship, the Half Moon.

Greene County

The Dutch were the first European settlers, arriving in the early part of the 17th century. Development took place along the Hudson River where the Dutch built several farmsteads. Today these early Dutch homes are historic and scenic attractions. The Bronck House is an excellent example and serves as the home of the Greene County Historical Society.

Depicted on the seal are the Hudson River and the Catskill Mountains.

Village of Catskill

"Rip Van Winkle" is a short story by American author Washington Irving, first published in 1819. Set just before the American Revolution, the character falls asleep in the Catskill Mountains for twenty years. He dreams of watching Henry Hudson and his crew playing 9-pins, and wakes up to find many changes in America and the Catskills. Interestingly, Irving wrote the story while living in England, and later claimed to have not ever been in the Catskills before he wrote it.

In addition to the natural beauty of the Catskills depicted in the seal, the Half Moon is shown sailing the waters of Rip Van Winkle's flowing beard while he sleeps.

Albany County

At the center of the seal is a silhouette of the Half Moon which references Henry Hudson's historic 1609 voyage and the Dutch character of the early settlement. The ship Half Moon is surrounded by winterberry, a local plant which represents the county's natural heritage. The county's incorporation date is 1683 and is one of the original counties of colonial New York.

Albany County Clerk Thomas Clingan was instrumental in the process of adopting a more appropriate seal than the earlier one, which did not reference the founding date. John Merril was the designer of the new seal, which was approved in 1995 by the State Legislature and then Governor George Pataki.

Town of Rensselaerville

The area now known as Rensselaerville was part of the huge Manor of Rensselaerwyck. The land was owned by the Dutch patroon, Kiliaen Van Rensselaer and his descendants. Settlement of the area did not take place until the late 1700s. The town was formed on March 8, 1790. Mills were very important to the farmers and settlers.

In the seal the town celebrates the grist mill that still exists, built in 1880 to replace previous mills on the site which had burned.

Town of Bethlehem

After Henry Hudson's journey in 1609, early settlement of the Town of Bethlehem began along the Hudson River. In 1649 the name Bethlehem referred to the settlement at the confluence of the Hudson and Vloman's Kill.

The seal was drawn by Alice Pauline Shafer and adopted by the Bethlehem Town Board in 1995. The figure of Henry Hudson and an illustration of his ship, the Half Moon, commemorate his arrival in 1609. Before him are flowers native to North America. The Mohawk Indian symbolizes the treaty to commemorate the beaver trade with the Dutch in 1617. Before him is a stalk of corn.

Town of New Scotland

The seal of the Town of New Scotland was drawn by Timothy Albright in 1975, winner of a contest sponsored by the Daughters of the American Revolution and the New Scotland Historical Society.

The windmill symbolizes the town's Dutch heritage; the thistle, the town's Scottish background. The mountains and ladder denote the Helderbergs and the Indians who lived there. A fire bush for Feura Bush is also included.

Town of Guilderland

While it is arguably the most Dutch of American municipal names, the Town of Guilderland has had at least four names through recorded history. In colonial times, it was part of the Manor of Rensselaerwyck, granted by the Dutch West India Company to Kiliaen Van Rensselaer in 1630. Settlers of Rensselaerwyck paid "quit rents" in the form of cash or "fat, fowl, wheat and labor" to permit them to clear land, construct buildings and grow crops.

In the 1700s, the area became known as the *Helleburgh* for the mountains in the southwest. This Dutch name meant "bright" or "clear mountains," and evolved to the current form of "Helderberg."

The area became part of the Town of Watervliet in 1778, and in 1803 it broke away to become the Town of Guilderland, with virtually the same boundaries it has today. The name "Guilderland" honored the province of Gelderland in the Netherlands, which was the homeland of the original settlers along the Normanskill.

The seal was adopted from the coat of arms of the Province of Gelderland, Holland, by permission granted in a letter dated March 11, 1959, and signed by the Commissioner of Queen Beatrix of the Netherlands. The English translation of the Latin motto on the riband is "Look Forward Guilderland."

Town of Colonie

The seal was officially adopted on May 8, 1941, and symbolizes the origin and background of the town. In the upper left hand quarter of the coat of arms is an American Indian, which represents the first inhabitants. In the upper right, the sheaf of wheat indicates the predominant occupation of the townspeople at the time the town was founded in 1895. In the lower left is a fort, which relates to the name of the town. *Colonie*, in Dutch, meant "the settlement outside the city," in this case, Fort Orange and Beverwyck. In the lower right quarter stands a windmill, signifying the Dutch heritage of the town's permanent settlers. Surrounding the four quarters is a circle of wampum, which represents the important Indian trade routes that passed through and bordered the town. The spray of laurel and sheaf of wheat signify a future of success and plenty.

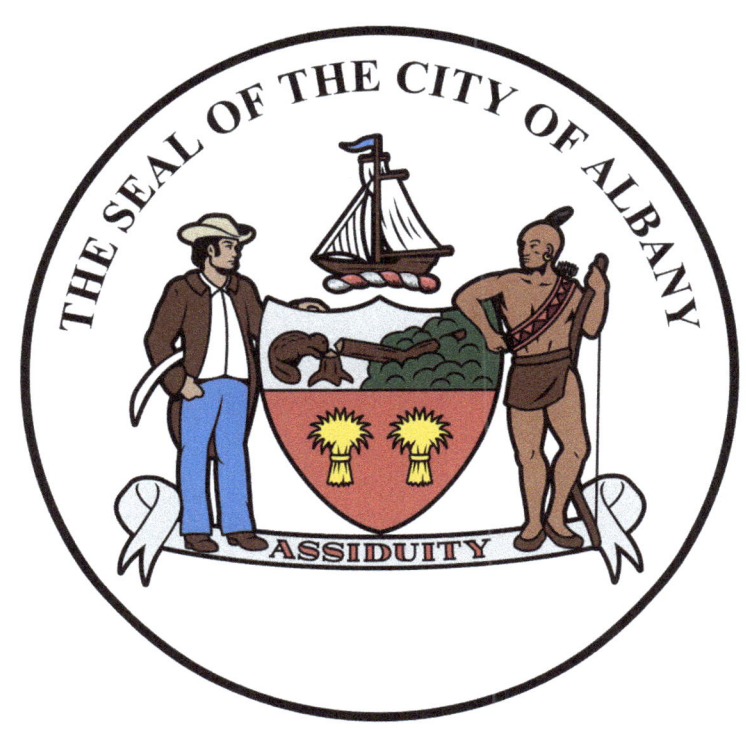

City of Albany

Albany was the second settlement in the thirteen original American colonies, after Jamestown, Virginia. The Dutch, who built a fort there in 1614, called the place "New Orange," after the Prince of Orange.

Beverwyck, "the home of the beaver," is the popular and mythical name given to the community of fur traders that first emerged along the river to the north of Fort Orange during the 1640s. The name came into official use in 1652 when the Dutch West India Company established a judicial jurisdiction for the land north of the trading post and fort. That act began a legacy of home rule for Albany that was primarily responsible for its development into a pre-urban center. Immediately following, the first house lots were parceled out. By the end of the decade, a log palisade had enclosed the settlement.

When the land was taken by the British in 1664, the name was changed to "Albany," in honor of the Duke of York and Albany, who later became James VII of Scotland and II of England. The Duke of Albany is a Scottish title given since 1398, generally to a younger son of the Scottish King. The name is derived from *Alba*, the Gaelic name for Scotland.

It was on July 22, 1686 that Governor Thomas Dongan, representing the British Crown, granted a charter recognizing Albany as a city. Dongan also appointed Pieter Schuyler as the first mayor. Since that time seventy-four men and one woman have served as mayor, of which thirty-four had Dutch heritage. Albany has the oldest effective city charter in the United States, and possibly in the entire Western Hemisphere.

The Arms of the City of Albany was first adopted pursuant to resolutions of the Common Council, passed on December 16, 1789 and January 9, 1790. The first Arms of the City were designed by Simeon DeWitt, who was an engineer on the staff of George Washington during the Revolution, City Surveyor of Albany, and Surveyor General of the State for nearly fifty years.

The Arms was later amended and readopted in 1887 by Chapter 44 of the General Ordinances of the City. The Arms illustrate the great history of Albany both before and after the Revolution.

The shield recognizes the value and importance of the city's two principal industries: fur trade and the manufacture of flour. The beaver, "resting on a tree stump which he is gnawing," has always been associated with Albany (*Beverwyck*). Albany was the beaver market of the world to both the Indian and trader who used beaver skins as money for barter. The other principal industry which provided Albany great wealth was the manufacture and trading of flour. The city's flour trade reached as far as the West Indies. The importance of flour is symbolized on the shield by two golden sheaves of wheat on a field.

The supporters of the shield, standing upon an extension of the scroll, represent a farmer of the Dutch colonial period and an American Indian, the men who produced the wealth symbolized on the shield.

The crest of the shield, a Dutch Hudson River sloop, under sail, underscores the value of shipping and commerce.

The city's motto, "Assiduity" appears on the scroll to indicate the dominant virtue of its citizens, that assiduous labor which "conquers all."

Examples of the Arms of the City of Albany as a subject for works of art appear on page 75.

City of Watervliet

Watervliet means "flowing water" in Dutch. The city is located along the banks of the Hudson River, just north of the City of Albany. Watervliet was originally known as the Village of West Troy and was incorporated on April 30, 1836.

The seal contains illustrations of the rising sun over the hills east of the Hudson, a sheaf of wheat and a cornucopia (to signify the bounty of the land), Robert Fulton's steamboat (the Clermont), and a Dutch sloop. The seal had its origins around the time the city was incorporated.

City of Cohoes

The City of Cohoes, located at the junction of the Mohawk and Hudson Rivers, was developed on land bought from the Indians in 1630 by Kiliaen Van Rensselaer, a director of the Dutch West India Company. Up to the time of the American Revolution, Cohoes was strictly an agricultural area. The seal represents a time later in the city's history as an industrial center. Unfortunately, the description and symbolism of the items depicted on the seal have been lost to history.

Rensselaer County

Rensselaer County was formed from Albany County on February 7, 1791. It was named for the vast Manor of Rensselaerwyck, owned by the first Patroon, Killian Van Rensselaer and his descendants. The official seal in use today is a simple outline drawing of the map of the county with towns.

Minutes from the first meeting in 1791 call for seal to be purchased with a drawing of "a plough and the words Seal of Rensselaer County." There are no further records of this seal.

The next seal found in the Gazetteer of the State of New York, published in 1860, has an illustration of a cornucopia. Some current seals with a cornucopia can still be found in the county building on 7th Street. The use of a cornucopia has been used to signify the plentiful bounty of nature.

Town of Schodack

The history of the development of the seal is not clear. Sometime before 1986, a contest was held by a Maple Hill School teacher named Connie Dodge. The winner was Ms. Mancini. This contest may have been held in conjunction with the country's bicentennial in 1976.

The image depicts a view across the Hudson River of the present day City of Albany, from a dock near where Henry Hudson landed in 1609, in what is now Castleton. A stylized illustration of Henry Hudson and his ship are superimposed on the scene.

The outer rim of the seal reflects the town's 200th anniversary in 1995, although the Town Clerk is sure the seal was in use before that time.

Town of Nassau

The seal was drawn by Martha Costello and Keith Prior and was adopted in September 2012 after more than a year of deciding to adopt a seal.

The main features include an eagle, with a flag signifying the Anti-Rent Wars of the 1800's and the role that the town and its citizens played. The illustration is a "Calico Indian." Local farmers dressed up as Indians similar to those who participated in the Boston Tea Party, and protested the feudal system of land ownership by the Van Rensselaer family since the 1600s. In the other claw are shafts of wheat symbolizing the agriculture of the town and a tin horn used by the farmers to warn neighboring farmers when tax collectors came for payment.

Below the eagle is a mill stone symbolizing the early industry of Nassau.

Village of Nassau

Jonathan Hoag settled in the area in 1792, and became the first Town Supervisor in 1807, when the Town of Nassau was organized. It was named "Philipstown," in honor of Philip Van Rensselaer. The village was christened "Union Village" in the early 1790s. The Village of Nassau was incorporated on March 12, 1819.

The seal illustrates an elm tree that Nassau was noted for, prior to their being destroyed by Dutch Elm disease.

Town of Stephentown

Originally a part of the Massachusetts Bay Colony, the town later became a part of the Manor of Rensselaerwyck. The shield represents the Van Rensselaer family Coat of Arms. Permission to put the family arms on the the seal was granted by Stephen Van Rensselaer, the great-great-grandson Stephen Van Rensselaer III.

The wording is arranged in a circle as a symbol of unity. The dividers are peaks depicting the Taconic and Petersburg ranges. The number of peaks denote the three hamlets of Stephentown, Stephentown Center, and West Stephentown.

Town of Sand Lake

The first permanent settlements in Sand Lake were made in its western part, probably in 1765 or 1766, by the descendants of Dutch settlers who had relocated from Albany or further down the Hudson Valley. The first two families were Adams and Brett (or Brandt). The majority of settlers that came later were mostly German and Scotch. Jeremiah Van Rensselaer founded the Rensselaer Glass Works in 1804, on land leased from the Patroon.

    The logo was designed by Patricia Brock and was chosen in May 1985 as a result of a contest. It depicts a large oak tree and the Town Hall (at the time), which was the former Sand Lake Presbyterian Church until 1967. The Town Hall, being in a former church, is reminiscent of the central role that religion has always played in the town. The oak tree represents the lumber business that was a part of the town's early history.

City of Rensselaer

The seal was designed by Ernie Mann with three themes in mind. Fort Crailo, built around 1712 by Hendrick Van Rensselaer, is the reputed location where "Yankee Doodle Dandy" was composed. A British Army surgeon, Dr. Richard Shuckburgh, sat on a well and wrote the derisive tune to mock the Colonial troops who fought with the British in the French and Indian Wars. The Half Moon represents Henry Hudson's voyage in 1609 and the subsequent Dutch settlement. The Patroon built a home in the place that later became the city. The railroad industry is symbolized by a locomotive. There were extensive rail yards in Rensselaer, and today it is home to one of the busiest Amtrak stations in the nation.

Town of North Greenbush

The town seal was chosen by the Town Board from a contest won by a second grader, possibly in conjunction with the country's bicentennial in 1976. The illustration features the Wynantskill Creek which flows through Wynantskill, where the town offices are located.

The Wynantskill was named after Wynant Gerritse Van Der Poel, part owner of a mill on the creek as of 1674. North Greenbush was carved out of a parcel of land granted to Patroon Stephen Van Rensselaer and became a town in 1855. *Greene Bosch* is a variant spelling of the Dutch term for "green bush," used to describe the landscape of the area.

Town of Poestenkill

During the 1660s, Jan Barentsen Wemp (also recorded as Jan Barentsen Poest in the early records of the colony) built a saw mill on the creek now referred to as the Poestenkill. The town thus derived its name from the creek, which flows through it. The town was incorporated in 1848.

In 1982 the town held a contest and chose the design of Barbara Woldt. It illustrates the creek, the broad-shouldered hills surrounding the town, and the churches which have been a part of the town since the early 1800s.

City of Troy

One of the earliest settlers was Derick Vanderheyden who obtained title to 490 acres in 1720. No records exist of the origin of the seal, however, the symbols depicted have been used on other seals before 1800 to indicate major trading goods, such as barrels of flour, bales of fur, and sheaves of wheat. In the background are illustrations of Dutch sloops used to transport goods on the Hudson River. The motto underneath, ILIUM FUIT TROJA EST, is Latin for "Ilium was, Troy is" (also translated as "Troy was, Troy is").

Town of Hoosick

The early settlers of the area were Dutch. Among the pioneer settlers was Jan Oothout who, prior to 1754, had built a home just inside the present boundaries of the Village of Hoosick Falls. Near the junction of the Little Hoosick and Hoosick rivers was a settlement known in colonial times as Hoosack. It lay between Hoosick Corners and North Petersburgh and was partly within the limits of the town of Petersburgh, and in the manor of Rensselaerwyck.

Town of Pittstown

The Town of Pittstown was given its name by King George III in 1761, in honor of the William Pitt, Earl of Chatham. The first settlers were of Dutch origin, occupying lands deeded to them by the Van Rensselaers. Early settlers were mainly farmers, bearing names such as Bleeker, Brant, Clark, Colden, De Peyster, Lansing, Sawyer, and Van Cortland, to mention a few.

The seal depicts an early settler plowing his fields against a backdrop of hills with a rising sun.

Town of Schaghticoke

The first permanent settler of record was Lewis Viele, son of Cornelise Viele of Schenectady, who moved to Schaghticoke in 1668. The first grant to lands in Schaghticoke was given to inhabitants of the city of Albany by the charter of 1686.

The seal dates from 1989, and commemorates the 1676 Witenagemot Council and depicts the Witenagemot Oak. The famous "Council Tree of Peace" was planted to strengthen the alliance between the Fort Albany militia and the Schaghticoke Indians. The white oak of the Schaghticokes lived until it was uprooted by the 1949 flood of the Hoosick River. Also depicted is a plow representing agriculture and a gear representing industry. Schaghticoke is the home of the Knickerbocker Family Mansion that dates from 1770, and is on the site of the Witenagemot Oak. The Knickerbocker family has been in Schaghticoke since 1709.

Village of Waterford

The simple seal of the Village of Waterford shows only a Dutch sloop under a half moon, but it speaks volumes of history.

In the 17th century Dutch traders and trappers first settled in Waterford, originally known as "Halfmoon" for the northernmost point of Hudson's 1609 voyage. When the village site was purchased in 1784 by Colonel Jacobus Van Schoonhoven and several others, settlement came rapidly. The village was incorporated in 1794, taking its name from the fording place on the Mohawk River, and is the oldest continually incorporated village in the United States.

Waterford lay at the head of sloop navigation on the Hudson River, and prospered from that trade when the Champlain and Erie Canals opened. At Waterford, sloop freight was loaded onto canal barges for transport, and the village became a major gateway to the canal system.

Town of Halfmoon

The Town of Halfmoon originally extended to Waterford and the Village of Waterford was known as Halfmoon, since that is as far as Henry Hudson could travel in 1609. In 1816 the old precinct of *Halve Maen* was divided into two separate towns, Waterford and Halfmoon. Clifton Park was removed as a separate town in 1828.

This is the logo rather than the official seal of the town, but it is used on the town vehicles and the official town web sites, including the Parks Department and others. The only illustration is a ship under full sail, representing Henry Hudson's ship the Half Moon, and the year that the town was established. There are also several variations of this design that are used on letterhead, the town's flag, and designs surrounding the entrances to the town buildings.

Town of Clifton Park

This seal emphasizes the heritage and history of the Town of Clifton Park and the area which it comprises. It contains several motifs, all of which are significant.

At the top of the shield are two flags which represent the two European nations which had a great deal of importance to the development of the town. On one side is the tricolor of the Netherlands, indicating the salience of the Dutch, while on the other is the Union Jack of Great Britain as it looked prior to the American Revolution.

The garland of corn sheaves is a tribute to the agricultural accomplishments of the the Indians, who called this area along the Mohawk River *Canastigione*, or "corn flats."

The garland of wheat on the opposite side of the seal is symbolic of the general importance of agriculture in the town's economy during the

19th and 20th centuries. More particularly, it denotes the significance of grain agriculture in this area.

In the middle of the shield is a constellation of five stars arranged in a semicircular pattern above a stylized half moon. These stars represent the five primary villages: Vischer Ferry (Amity), Jonesville (Elnora), Clifton Park (the town's namesake), Grooms Corners, and Rexford Flats. The half moon represents the recognition of the town's inclusion from 1791 to 1828 in the Town of Halfmoon, and Clifton Park's emergence from the same town.

The stylized portrayal of the Mohawk River is representative of the Mohawk's importance of transportation and agriculture to the growth and development of Clifton Park.

The ribbon with the date "1828" is wrapped about both external garlands and winds upward, while its movement ending above the shield represents upward growth and prosperity.

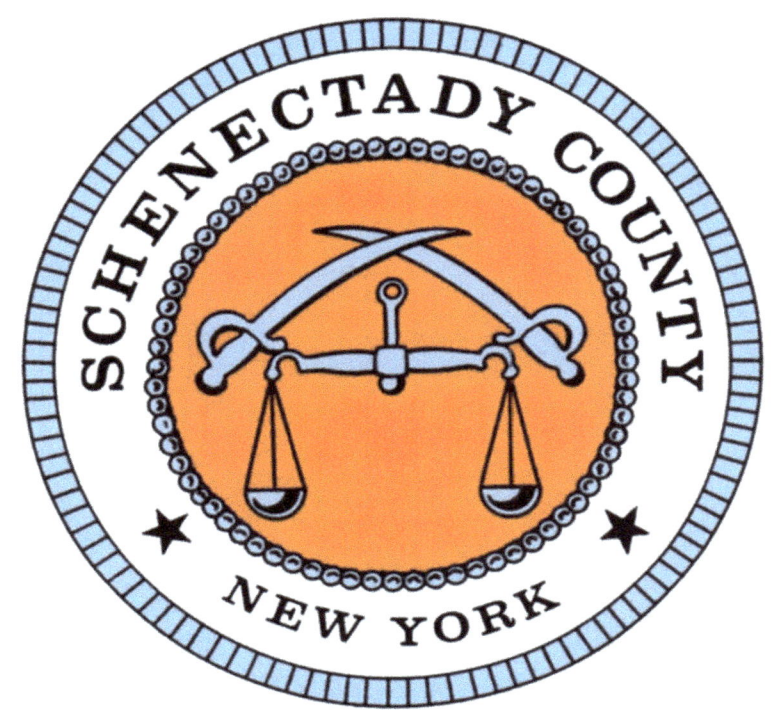

Schenectady County

In June, 1661, Arendt Van Curler and fourteen others applied to Dutch Governor Peter Stuyvesant for permission to purchase from the Mohawk Indians the "Great Flat," a tract of land on the lower Mohawk. The earliest European settlers of Schenectady County came from the Netherlands.

The name Schenectady is believed to derive from the Iroquois word *Schau-naugh-ta-da*, which translated to "the place beyond the pines." It was said to refer to the place where Schenectady now stands, across the pine barrens from Albany, the earlier Dutch settlement.

Schenectady County was incorporated on March 7, 1809. The seal depicts a set of scales beneath crossed swords, representing strength and justice. The colors (blue and orange) were borrowed from the colonial Dutch flag.

Town of Niskayuna

The seal was designed by area resident Robert Banks for the nation's bicentennial and was adopted in 1976. The town was established in 1809.

The upper right side depicts an Indian holding an ear of corn. The tepees in the background represent the Iroquois Nations. The word *niskayuna* means "land of extended corn fields." The lower right portrays a Shaker farmer. The Shakers named their first community after the Indian word (though it was actually in Watervliet). The canal boat in the upper left represents the Erie Canal's importance to the town. At lower left is the atomic symbol, depicted for the modern nuclear industry in Niskayuna. In the center is a geographic outline of the town, with some typical farm crops placed below the letter "N" in stonework.

City of Schenectady

Arent Van Curler, along with fourteen other Dutch landholders, settled along the Mohawk in 1661 on a piece of land that eventually became the City of Schenectady. The area they settled is now known as the Stockade Historic District. It was the first established in New York State, and is considered to be the oldest residential neighborhood in the country, with more than 40 homes over 200 years old. The stockaded village was completely burned by a raiding party of French and Indians in 1690, but was rebuilt in 1692.

In 1765, Schenectady was incorporated as a borough. It was chartered as a city in 1798. The City Seal was engraved in 1800 at a cost of $11.00, as described by the Schenectady Historical Society. The shock of wheat recalls the early agricultural settlement of the Stockade and symbolizes peace and plenty. The colors orange and blue are from the Dutch flag.

Town of Rotterdam

Rotterdam was first settled predominately by the Dutch, following the establishment of the settlement at present day Schenectady. The town, named after the City of Rotterdam in the Netherlands, was formed from a ward of the City of Schenectady on April 14, 1820. The Coat of Arms of the Town of Rotterdam was granted in 1952 by the government of the Netherlands.

Rotterdam is home to the oldest house in the Mohawk Valley, the Mabee Farm, originally settled by Daniel Janse Van Antwerpen around 1670, who established it as a fur-trading post to meet Iroquois and Mohawk traders before they reached Schenectady. In 1705 the property was sold to Jan Mabee and remained in the Mabee family for 300 years. Now a state Historic Site with additional Dutch and English barns and other structures, it tells the history of the Dutch influence in Schenectady County.

Village of Scotia

In 1658, Alexander Lindsey of Glen bought land along the Mohawk River from the Iroquois Indians. He was an agent of the Dutch East India Company who emigrated to the New World with Dutch settlers, but he named his estate *Nova Scotia*, in memory of his native Scotland. His standing with the French in Canada was to prove fortuitous, as his home and family were spared during the Stockade Massacre of 1690, carried out by a raiding party of French and their Indian allies.

After the original stone house (depicted in the seal) was flooded, his son John Glen built a one-room dwelling, which is now the kitchen of the current Glen Sanders Mansion. He later expanded the building with a Dutch gambrel roof, still intact as well.

City of Amsterdam

Located west of Schenectady on the Mohawk River, Amsterdam was named for the city in Holland where many early settlers came from. Originally called "Veedersburgh" after one of the first settlers, Albert Veeder, the city was incorporated on April 20, 1830.

The city has a long history of industrialization from its abundant water supply. The seal is an updated version of a windmill, drawn by a local bussinessman, Robert Olbrycht, in 2009.

Seals as Subjects for Works of Art

Many municipal seals have been reproduced in stained glass, bronze, or even granite, as seen here with the Coat of Arms of the City of Albany. In one very unique case, the seal was rendered in a three-dimensional sculpture. It was done by noted political cartoonist Hy Rosen, who retired in 1989 from the *Albany Times-Union* after a career of 44 years. The 6'4" sculpture stands in Tricentennial Park on Broadway in downtown Albany. In nearly every instance, artistic liberty was taken and minor changes from the official seal are observed.

Acknowledgments

To make it easier for the reader, this list of source acknowledgments is arranged alphabetically by municipality, as opposed to the arrangement of the content within the book.

Since the First Edition of this book was published in 2009, the people listed here may no longer be in office. The author wishes to acknowledge their help with images or history or both.

Albany, City of: John Marsolais, City Clerk; Archives of the Albany Institute of History and Art; Albany Public Library; the New York State Public Library.

Albany, County of: Jill Hughes, County Records; Hon. Thomas G Clingan, County Clerk.

Amsterdam, City of: Robert H. von Hasseln, City Historian.

Bethlehem, Town of: Kathleen Newkirk, Town Clerk.

The Bronx, Borough of: Magali Iglesais, Deputy Press Secretary, Assistant to the Communications Director, Office of the the Bronx Borough President.

Brooklyn, Borough of: *www.Brooklyn-usa.org*.

Catskill, Village of: Carolyn S. Pardy, Clerk, Treasurer.

Clavarack, Town of: *www.townofclaverack.com*.

Clifton Park, Town of: Pat O'Donnell, Town Clerk.

Cohoes, City of: City Hall.

Colonie, Town of: Kevin Franklin, Town Historian.

Columbia, County of: Holly C. Tanner, Columbia County Clerk; Mary Howell, Historian; Alex Cox, Deputy Clerk, Board of Supervisors.

Dutchess, County of: *www.dutchessny.gov*.

Fishkill, Town of: Willa Skinner, Town Historian.

Greene, County of: Tracy Spitz, Administrative Assistant; Carol Stevens, County Attorney.

Guilderland, Town of: Alice Begley, Town Historian; Guilderland Chamber of Commerce.

Halfmoon, Town of: Mary Pearson, Town Clerk.

Haverstraw, Town of: Josephine Carella; *www.townofhaverstraw.org*.

Hoosick, Town of: Susan Stradinger, Town Clerk.

Hudson, City of: Bonita Colwell, City Clerk; Alberta H. Cox, Deputy Clerk, Columbia County Board of Supervisors.

Hyde Park, Town of: Carole Clearwater, Town Clerk; Pompey Delafield, Town Supervisor.

Kinderhook, Town of: Kim Pinkowski, Town Clerk.

Kingston, City of: *ci.kingston.ny.us*.

Manhattan, Borough of: Wikipedia; Wikimedia Commons.

Nassau, County of: *www.nassaucountyny.gov*.

Nassau, Town of: Diane Maguire, Historic Preservation.

Nassau, Village of: Margaret Van Deusen, Treasurer.

New Scotland, Town of: Diane Deschenes, Town Clerk.

New York, City of: Mark Daly, Director of Communications, Department of Citywide Administration.

Niskayuna, Town of: Helen Kopke, Town Clerk; *History of Niskayuna, New York* (Harder and Johnson, editors).

North Greenbush, Town of: Kathryn Connolly, Town Clerk; *Landmarks of Rensselaer County* (George Anderson, 1897).

Orange, County of: Pat Weber, Office of the Orange County Historian.

Oyster Bay, Town of: *www.oysterbaytown.com*.

Peekskill, City of: *www.cityofpeekskill.com*.

Pittstown, Town of: Michelle Hoag, Town Clerk.

Poestenkill, Town of: *www.poestenkillny.com*.

Poughkeepsie, City of: Deanne Flynn, City Chamberlain.

Queens Borough of: Roslyn Liturri, Press Office.

Rensselaer, City of: Dan Dwyer, Mayor; Ernie Mann.

Rensselaer, County of: Jenet Marra, Clerk of the Legislature; Christine Chesley, Director of Governmental Relations.

Rensselaerville, Town of: Kathleen Hallenbeck, Town Clerk.

Rhinebeck, Town of: Barb Cunningham, Town Clerk; Nancy Kelly, Town Historian.

Rockland, County of: *www.rocklandgov.com*.

Rotterdam, Town of: Eunice Esposito, Town Clerk.

Sand Lake, Town of: *Landmarks of Rensselaer County* (George Anderson, 1897); Sand Lake Historical Society.

Saugerties, Village of: *www.saugerties.ny.us*.

Schaghticoke, Town of: Janet Salisbury, Town Clerk; Jean Carlson, Town Supervisor.

Schenectady, City of: *www.cityofschenectady.com*; *www.historicstockade.com*.

Schenectady, County of: *www.schenectadycounty.com*.

Schodack, Town of: Diane L. Hutchinson, Town Historian.

Scotia, Village of: *www.glensandersmansion.com*.

Sleepy Hollow, Village of: Anthony P. Giaccio, Village Administrator; Henry Steiner, Village Historian.

Staten Island, Borough of: Thomas Matteo, Staten Island Historian; Cara Dellatte, Archivist.

Stephentown, Town of: Beverly McClave, Stephentown Historical Society.

Stuyvesant, Town of: Valerie Bertram, Town Supervisor; Melissa Naegeli, Town Clerk; *History of Columbia County, New York* (Ellis Franklin, 1878).

Tarrytown, Village of: Carol Booth, Town Clerk; Richard Miller, Village Historian.

Troy, City of: Donna Ned, Senior Planning Technician; Kathy Sheehan, Rensselaer County Historical Society.

Ulster, County of: Vincent C. Martello, Assistant Deputy County Executive.

Valatie, Village of: Dominick Lizzi, Village Historian.

Watervliet, City of: Mike Manning, Mayor; Paul Murphy, Historian.

Yonkers, City of: *www.cityofyonkers.com*.

About the Author

Marvin Bubie was born and raised in the Capital District, graduating from Averill Park High School and Rensselaer Polytechnic Institute. He is retired from General Electric and has lived in New Jersey, Pennsylvania, Georgia, and Virginia. In addition, he spent eighteen months in Germany with the US Army, and has returned to Europe many times visiting Switzerland, Italy, Austria, and Germany. Over the years he has collected the seals of various cities, towns, counties, boroughs, and villages in this country, as well as those in Europe. He has published two similar books, *Along the Erie Canal with the Municipal Seals of the Cities, Towns and Villages of New York*, and *Celebrating the American Revolution: Municipal Symbols of a Free Country*, and is at work on another book of seals related to railroading heritage.

www.ingramcontent.com/pod-product-compliance
Lightning Source LLC
Chambersburg PA
CBHW061414090426
42742CB00023B/3462